THE ENCYCLOPEDIA OF PSYCHOACTIVE DRUGS

DRUGS
&
THE FAMILY

GENERAL EDITOR
Professor Solomon H. Snyder, M.D.

*Distinguished Service Professor of
Neuroscience, Pharmacology, and Psychiatry at
The Johns Hopkins University School of Medicine*

•

ASSOCIATE EDITOR
Professor Barry L. Jacobs, Ph.D.

*Program in Neuroscience, Department of Psychology,
Princeton University*

•

SENIOR EDITORIAL CONSULTANT
Joann Rodgers

*Deputy Director, Office of Public Affairs at
The Johns Hopkins Medical Institutions*

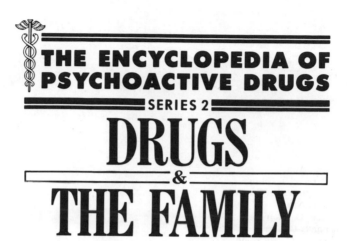

THE ENCYCLOPEDIA OF PSYCHOACTIVE DRUGS

SERIES 2

DRUGS
&
THE FAMILY

JO MARTIN & KELLY CLENDENON

CHELSEA HOUSE PUBLISHERS

NEW YORK • NEW HAVEN • PHILADELPHIA

EDITOR-IN-CHIEF: Nancy Toff
EXECUTIVE EDITOR: Remmel T. Nunn
MANAGING EDITOR: Karyn Gullen Browne
COPY CHIEF: Juliann Barbato
PICTURE EDITOR: Adrian G. Allen
ART DIRECTOR: Giannella Garrett
MANUFACTURING MANAGER: Gerald Levine

Staff for DRUGS AND THE FAMILY:

SENIOR EDITOR: Jane Larkin Crain
ASSOCIATE EDITOR: Paula Edelson
ASSISTANT EDITOR: Laura-Ann Dolce
EDITORIAL ASSISTANT: Susan DeRosa
COPY EDITOR: Gillian Bucky, James Guiry
ASSOCIATE PICTURE EDITOR: Juliette Dickstein
DESIGNER: Victoria Tomaselli
DESIGN ASSISTANT: Donna Sinisgalli
PRODUCTION COORDINATOR: Joseph Romano
COVER ILLUSTRATION: Nava Atlas

CREATIVE DIRECTOR: Harold Steinberg

First Printing

1 3 5 7 9 8 6 4 2

Library of Congress Cataloging in Publication Data

Martin, Jo.
  Drugs & the family.
  (The Encyclopedia of psychoactive drugs. Series 2)
  Bibliography: p.
  Summary: Discusses the effects of drug use, from the start, through addiction,
to the beginning of the road back to normal health.
    1. Youth—United States—Drug use—Prevention—Juvenile literature. 2. Drug
abuse—United States—Prevention—Juvenile literature. [1. Drug abuse]
I. Clendenon, Kelly. II. Title. III. Title: Drugs and the family. IV. Series.
HV5824.Y68M367 1988   362.2'93   87-24258

ISBN 1-55546-220-0

CONTENTS

FOREWORD

In the Mainstream
of American Life

One of the legacies of the social upheaval of the 1960s is that psychoactive drugs have become part of the mainstream of American life. Schools, homes, and communities cannot be "drug proofed." There is a demand for drugs — and the supply is plentiful. Social norms have changed and drugs are not only available—they are everywhere.

But where efforts to curtail the supply of drugs and outlaw their use have had tragically limited effects on demand, it may be that education has begun to stem the rising tide of drug abuse among young people and adults alike.

Over the past 25 years, as drugs have become an increasingly routine facet of contemporary life, a great many teenagers have adopted the notion that drug taking was somehow a right or a privilege or a necessity. They have done so, however, without understanding the consequences of drug use during the crucial years of adolescence.

The teenage years are few in the total life cycle, but critical in the maturation process. During these years adolescents face the difficult tasks of discovering their identity, clarifying their sexual roles, asserting their independence, learning to cope with authority, and searching for goals that will give their lives meaning.

Drugs rob adolescents of precious time, stamina, and health. They interrupt critical learning processes, sometimes forever. Teenagers who use drugs are likely to withdraw increasingly into themselves, to "cop out" at just the time when they most need to reach out and experience the world.

Fortunately, as a recent Gallup poll shows, young people are beginning to realize this, too. They themselves label drugs their most important problem. In the last few years, moreover, the climate of tolerance and ignorance surrounding drugs has been changing.

Adolescents as well as adults are becoming aware of mounting evidence that every race, ethnic group, and class is vulnerable to drug dependency.

Recent publicity about the cost and failure of drug rehabilitation efforts; dangerous drug use among pilots, air traffic controllers, star athletes, and Hollywood celebrities; and drug-related accidents, suicides, and violent crime have focused the public's attention on the need to wage an all-out war on drug abuse before it seriously undermines the fabric of society itself.

The anti-drug message is getting stronger and there is evidence that the message is beginning to get through to adults and teenagers alike.

The Encyclopedia of Psychoactive Drugs hopes to play a part in the national campaign now underway to educate young people about drugs. Series 1 provides clear and comprehensive discussions of common psychoactive substances, outlines their psychological and physiological effects on the mind and body, explains how they "hook" the user, and separates fact from myth in the complex issue of drug abuse.

Whereas Series 1 focuses on specific drugs, such as nicotine or cocaine, Series 2 confronts a broad range of both social and physiological phenomena. Each volume addresses the ramifications of drug use and abuse on some aspect of human experience: social, familial, cultural, historical, and physical. Separate volumes explore questions about the effects of drugs on brain chemistry and unborn children; the use and abuse of painkillers; the relationship between drugs and sexual behavior, sports, and the arts; drugs and disease; the role of drugs in history; and the sophisticated drugs now being developed in the laboratory that will profoundly change the future.

Each book in the series is fully illustrated and is tailored to the needs and interests of young readers. The more adolescents know about drugs and their role in society, the less likely they are to misuse them.

Joann Rodgers
Senior Editorial Consultant

INTRODUCTION

The Gift of Wizardry
Use and Abuse

JACK H. MENDELSON, M.D.
NANCY K. MELLO, Ph.D.
Alcohol and Drug Abuse Research Center
Harvard Medical School—McLean Hospital

Dorothy to the Wizard:

"I think you are a very bad man," said Dorothy.
"Oh no, my dear; I'm really a very good man; but I'm a very bad Wizard."
—from THE WIZARD OF OZ

Man is endowed with the gift of wizardry, a talent for discovery and invention. The discovery and invention of substances that change the way we feel and behave are among man's special accomplishments, and, like so many other products of our wizardry, these substances have the capacity to harm as well as to help. Psychoactive drugs can cause profound changes in the chemistry of the brain and other vital organs, and although their legitimate use can relieve pain and cure disease, their abuse leads in a tragic number of cases to destruction.

Consider alcohol — available to all and yet regarded with intense ambivalence from biblical times to the present day. The use of alcoholic beverages dates back to our earliest ancestors. Alcohol use and misuse became associated with the worship of gods and demons. One of the most powerful Greek gods was Dionysus, lord of fruitfulness and god of wine. The Romans adopted Dionysus but changed his name to Bacchus. Festivals and holidays associated with Bacchus celebrated the harvest and the origins of life. Time has blurred the images of the Bacchanalian festival, but the theme of drunkenness as a major part of celebration has survived the pagan gods and remains a familiar part of modern society. The term "Bacchanalian Festival" conveys a more appealing image than "drunken orgy" or "pot party," but whatever the label, drinking alcohol is a form of drug use that results in addiction for millions.

The fact that many millions of other people can use alcohol in moderation does not mitigate the toll this drug takes on society as a whole. According to reliable estimates, one out of every ten Americans develops a serious alcohol-related problem sometime in his or her lifetime. In addition, automobile accidents caused by drunken drivers claim the lives of tens of thousands every year. Many of the victims are gifted young people, just starting out in adult life. Hospital emergency rooms abound with patients seeking help for alcohol-related injuries.

Who is to blame? Can we blame the many manufacturers who produce such an amazing variety of alcoholic beverages? Should we blame the educators who fail to explain the perils of intoxication, or so exaggerate the dangers of drinking that no one could possibly believe them? Are friends to blame — those peers who urge others to "drink more and faster," or the macho types who stress the importance of being able to "hold your liquor"? Casting blame, however, is hardly constructive, and pointing the finger is a fruitless way to deal with the problem. Alcoholism and drug abuse have few culprits but many victims. Accountability begins with each of us, every time we choose to use or misuse an intoxicating substance.

It is ironic that some of man's earliest medicines, derived from natural plant products, are used today to poison and to intoxicate. Relief from pain and suffering is one of society's many continuing goals. Over 3,000 years ago, the Therapeutic Papyrus of Thebes, one of our earliest written records, gave instructions for the use of opium in the treatment of pain. Opium, in the form of its major derivative, morphine, and similar compounds, such as heroin, have also been used by many to induce changes in mood and feeling. Another example of man's misuse of a natural substance is the coca leaf, which for centuries was used by the Indians of Peru to reduce fatigue and hunger. Its modern derivative, cocaine, has important medical use as a local anesthetic. Unfortunately, its increasing abuse in the 1980s clearly has reached epidemic proportions.

The purpose of this series is to explore in depth the psychological and behavioral effects that psychoactive drugs have on the individual, and also, to investigate the ways in which drug use influences the legal, economic, cultural, and even moral aspects of societies. The information presented here (and in other books in this series) is based on many clinical and laboratory studies and other observations by people from diverse walks of life.

Over the centuries, novelists, poets, and dramatists have provided us with many insights into the sometimes seductive but ultimately problematic aspects of alcohol and drug use. Physicians, lawyers, biologists, psychologists, and social scientists have contributed to a better understanding of the causes and consequences of using these substances. The authors in this series have attempted to gather and condense all the latest information about drug use and abuse. They have also described the sometimes wide gaps in our knowledge and have suggested some new ways to answer many difficult questions.

One such question, for example, is how do alcohol and drug problems get started? And what is the best way to treat them when they do? Not too many years ago, alcoholics and drug abusers were regarded as evil, immoral, or both. It is now recognized that these persons suffer from very complicated diseases involving deep psychological and social problems. To understand how the disease begins and progresses, it is necessary to understand the nature of the substance, the behavior of addicts, and the characteristics of the society or culture in which they live.

Although many of the social environments we live in are very similar, some of the most subtle differences can strongly influence our thinking and behavior. Where we live, go to school and work, whom we discuss things with — all influence our opinions about drug use and misuse. Yet we also share certain commonly accepted beliefs that outweigh any differences in our attitudes. The authors in this series have tried to identify and discuss the central, most crucial issues concerning drug use and misuse.

Despite the increasing sophistication of the chemical substances we create in the laboratory, we have a long way to go in our efforts to make these powerful drugs work for us rather than against us.

The volumes in this series address a wide range of timely questions. What influence has drug use had on the arts? Why do so many of today's celebrities and star athletes use drugs, and what is being done to solve this problem? What is the relationship between drugs and crime? What is the physiological basis for the power drugs can hold over us? These are but a few of the issues explored in this far-ranging series.

Educating people about the dangers of drugs can go a long way towards minimizing the desperate consequences of substance abuse for individuals and society as a whole. Luckily, human beings have the resources to solve even the most serious problems that beset them, once they make the commitment to do so. As one keen and sensitive observer, Dr. Lewis Thomas, has said,

> There is nothing at all absurd about the human condition. We matter. It seems to me a good guess, hazarded by a good many people who have thought about it, that we may be engaged in the formation of something like a mind for the life of this planet. If this is so, we are still at the most primitive stage, still fumbling with language and thinking, but infinitely capacitated for the future. Looked at this way, it is remarkable that we've come as far as we have in so short a period, really no time at all as geologists measure time. We are the newest, youngest, and the brightest thing around.

DRUGS
&
THE FAMILY

CHAPTER 1

GETTING ACQUAINTED

We're going to spend some time together, so let me make the introductions.

My son is a drug addict. That's the first thing you should know.

If a stranger asked me to describe Kelly, that's what I'd say. Then I'd mention that he's 16, he's smart, he likes most sports, he's tall and good looking (although he doesn't think so), he talks a lot about girls and cars, and he wants to be an architect or graphic designer.

I'd mention drugs first because Kelly's addiction controlled our family like a tyrant for nearly two years. It still has a lot to do with how we spend our time. We spend two evenings a week in counseling sessions, we've been to our share of Narcotics Anonymous meetings, and we have written this book. Addiction can take hold in a matter of months; recovery in its various stages can take years.

Our family life is more or less back in balance now, but for a long time all our energy went into worrying about Kelly — would he be able to get up in the morning? what kind of mood would he be in? would the principal call to say that Kelly wasn't in school again? would he come home in the evening? It was the same thing day after day.

For a long time we didn't know Kelly was taking drugs. We thought the changes in his personality were part of the emotional turmoil of early adolescence. Eventually, we knew there was much more to it. His behavior became erratic and he sometimes couldn't remember things. His self-esteem eroded, and he became apathetic and withdrawn.

To be honest, we didn't like Kelly much during that time. It hurts when you don't like your own child. When he was being selfish and dishonest — which is what addicts are — we sometimes didn't care what happened to him because we resented how his choices were swallowing us up. And then we hated ourselves for being selfish in our own way. We felt Kelly's addiction slowly poisoning our family, and we made some painful decisions to take charge again.

That brings me to the second thing you should know. Kelly spent seven months in a psychiatric hospital trying to overcome his addiction and trying to figure out why he was attracted to drugs like marijuana, LSD, and speed. That takes a lot of guts. In the weeks before he went into the hospital, Kelly came and went as he pleased from our Baltimore home. He was disrespectful and rebellious, convinced he could take charge of his life. We were simply too drained emotionally to try to reason with him. It was a battle we had lost before and were sick and tired of fighting.

The day he went into the hospital, the staff made him take the earring out of his left earlobe. Then they took him down a long hall. Before he walked through the doorway, he turned around to smile shyly at us. The face was that of the little boy I had known years before. Then the door closed and locked behind him.

We couldn't see him or talk to him for two weeks. In the months that followed, we never knew what he would be like when we rang the bell on the waiting room door.

Having Kelly gone was hell and heaven. The house was quiet again and the family began to heal. Yet we ached to have him back, without the temper tantrums and tension.

In a nutshell, this book is about drug addiction and the toll it takes on everyone it touches. The addict himself is not the only victim. His disease infects every life entwined with his own.

That's why you need to know the rest of us. I'm Kelly's mom and we have a close relationship, but sometimes we can't stand to be in the same room. He says I'm too much like the mother on "Leave It to Beaver" and I say he should be glad he comes from a family that cares enough about him to have rules. We fight now and then — at meals, among other times — because he's a normal teenager and I'm a normal mom in her early 40s. I want him to do well. He wants to be left alone.

Kelly has a sister who is 11. Her name is Jessica, and she is an example of how addiction hurt our family. It was tough for a little kid to see her big brother change as much as Kelly did. I'm sure she has fears that what happened to him could happen to her. She saw how much my husband and I worried about Kelly, and she had to live with the fact that often we didn't have time to spend with her because we were preoccupied with her brother. We have a lot of catching up to do with Jess.

Kelly's father and I were divorced when Kelly was six. Our divorce was not malicious, but it still caused a great deal of suffering. The biggest hurt was Kelly's. His dad told me he wanted a divorce when Jessica was a few months old, so Kelly lost a father and gained a little sister at about the same time. That's a big change for a child and I always will regret that I couldn't do more to lessen the pain for Kelly.

It's even possible that, in part, Kelly was attracted to drugs as a way of cushioning the feelings he still has about his father and our separation.

I married Curtis Martin in 1985. I was a single mother for seven years and I met Curtis right after my divorce. The first time Kelly met Curtis he asked if we could adopt him. But as Kelly got older, he began to resent my relationship with Curtis. Kelly wanted to be the only man in my life.

When the psychiatrist interviewed Kelly the day he was admitted to the hospital, he asked him about our wedding. Kelly replied, "It was something I made up my mind to endure." That was news to us since he was our best man. We later learned that the day we told the kids we were getting married, it was just one more time Kelly hid his real feelings. He told us he was happy for us, took his clothes out of the dryer, went to a friend's house, and got high.

A general statement about my family is hard to make since my opinion about them changes each day.

Generally, I feel my relationship with my family is strong. I fight with my little sister, but that's normal. And so are a lot of other things that go on in our house — like disagreements over rules, homework, and who does what chores. One thing that's *different* is that we all care a great deal about each other. Don't get me wrong. I know other families care a lot about each other. But I bet that a lot more don't.

My mother and father were divorced about ten years ago, when I was six, so I was raised by my mom and learned to become independent at a young age. When I say I became independent, I mean I learned to get along with people older than myself at a younger age. Also, I learned to do things like make snacks, make my bed, etc. In some ways, I'm glad I'm independent, but in other ways, I'm not. At times I can make myself think that I can handle the world, but that puts a tremendous load of pressure on my shoulders. Maybe I'm not as emotionally independent as I'd like to think I am.

I have a stepfather now, and I just started to get along better with him, but it's a slow process. My sister and I never got along well. My parents say she really loves me, which I believe sometimes. I think that behind all the fighting we both love each other.

My dad lives in Pittsburgh, and we live in Baltimore. He has lived all over the place, and he also has been through treatment for drug abuse. We have a lot in common and can relate to each other. I only see him on holidays and for a week in the summer. I wish I could see him more often.

Finally, there's my mom. I love my mom to death and we get along most of the time. But we think differently, which can cause problems. I think she sees a lot of my father in me.

As for me, I'm basically a well-known guy around where we live. I don't have a lot of enemies because I'm not the type of person who goes around looking for trouble. That may sound strange coming from someone who got in so far over his head with drugs, but I never saw smoking pot or tripping on acid as a way to cause trouble. It always seemed like a way to cope with problems, not create them.

I always thought I was addicted only to drugs, but if I really look at it I'm addicted to just about everything that looks me in the face. That includes food and girls. I guess you could say, in a way, I'm infatuated with girls. Actually,

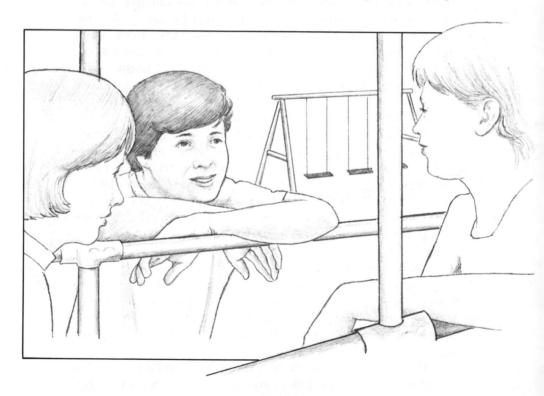

that has been an issue raised many times with my therapist and family. I can sometimes substitute girls for security. I did that more before than now. I'd say I have a normal teenage love life now. I'm your average horny 16-year-old.

I want everything to come easy. All I had to do with drugs was smoke them or swallow them and sit back. It was too easy.

I've changed a lot in the past few years. I used to be shy and insecure. Now I talk too much. I used to stay around the house, but now a night at home with my family gets me on edge. Sometimes I wonder if I've changed for the better. I guess some of the changes are for the better and some aren't.

One of the things my mom worried about when she was divorced was that I'd be gay because I was being raised by a woman. I proved her wrong. Now she's worried I like girls too much.

I'm just a laid-back guy with an uptight family. I don't want to make it sound like I hate them. It's just that our views differ on most things. I guess most kids my age have mixed feelings about their families, resenting being bossed around one minute, glad for their support the next. But in my case, at least, the good outweighs the bad. Overall, I love and care about my family.

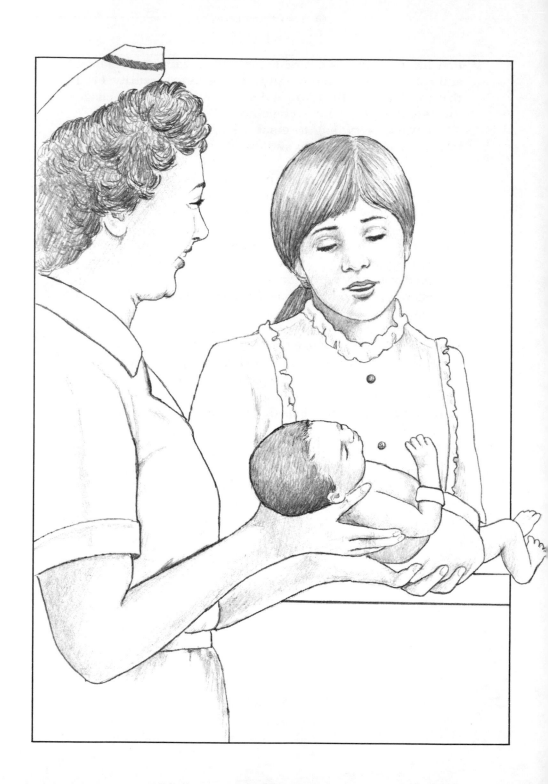

CHAPTER 2

THE START

Kelly takes drugs to soften life. I know that because we've spent nearly two years talking to psychiatrists, psychologists, and social workers about his drug problem. They have helped us see the connection among his personality, events he couldn't control, and his desire for drugs.

This will probably embarrass Kelly, but I'm going to tell you some important things about his childhood. It will help set the stage for how he became a drug addict.

Kelly was born at 6:10 A.M. on March 5, 1971, in Ft. Lauderdale, Florida. I don't know what happens to the human brain when it anticipates that something important is going on, but I remember each part of that day vividly. There are details I will never forget.

What sticks out in my mind is that it took me four hours to get up the nerve to walk to the nursery to look at my son for the first time. I can't explain it. The anesthesia from the delivery made me sleepy so all I knew was that I had a son and he was healthy.

Seeing my first child for the first time was the most important moment in my life. I was overwhelmed. There he was, sandy brown hair, eyes closed tight, throwing up all over the nurse as she changed his diaper. He was gorgeous.

When Kelly was three months old, we moved to Washington, D.C. This was a terrific locale because most of my family lived in nearby Baltimore.

Kel's dad worked nights and some weekends in the sports department of a major newspaper. He slept during the day, so Kel and I were together a lot, and we had to find things to do so we wouldn't disturb his dad. We often took long rides. I remember cruising around the Virginia countryside singing Stevie Wonder's "You Are the Sunshine of My Life" to the chubby little kid in the car seat next to me.

I didn't have to go to work. I was a full-time mom and Kelly had my undivided attention.

When Kelly was two, I enrolled him in a preschool because he was extremely shy and there were no children for him to play with in our neighborhood. For the first few weeks he screamed when I drove him up to the school each morning. I felt mean making him get out of the car, but I knew it was important for him to be with other children.

There are two things about Kelly that didn't change until much later. He stayed shy and he stayed chubby. That can be a tough combination for a sensitive kid.

When Kel was five his dad got a job at a newspaper in Chicago. I was pregnant with Jessica and we had to sell our house before all of us could move, so Kel and I stayed behind when his dad went to Chicago. He left on March 6, 1976, one day after Kelly's birthday. We saw him only twice in the next four months.

After we moved to Chicago things didn't go well for Kelly's dad and me. In less than two years we were divorced, so the kids and I moved to Baltimore to be near my relatives.

It was tough for Kelly. He missed his dad and his dog. And for the first time I had to go to work. All at once, he was getting used to a new city, new friends, a new school, and an almost-new sister. On top of that, a babysitter was waiting for him after school now. It was also about that time that I started dating Curtis, one of my friends from work.

During the first few years after the divorce, Kelly didn't have a lot of self-esteem, but he had a few close friends and did well in school. I found a psychologist for him just so he would have an ongoing relationship with a man. They visited once a week for about eight months. Sometimes they'd take long walks, and other times they'd sit together in the psychologist's office. Kelly needed someone to talk with about his feelings about the divorce, because he thought maybe it was something he had caused.

There were times when Kel was alone after school and he was frightened. Babysitters we found were unreliable. Once, I needed a sitter for all day because Kel had a day off from school. The night before, she canceled, and I had to stay at home. Another time, the sitter took Jessica for a walk in the park but didn't tell Kelly where they were going. He called me up at work in a panic and I had to come home. After all, he was only 10 or 11. Sometimes when he was by himself, Kelly carried a knife around the apartment in case an imagined stranger tried to get in.

There was only one time in those years when Kelly forcefully let out his feelings. He asked me for something and I said he couldn't have it, so he kicked a hole in the wall of our dining room. I was stunned, but he seemed relieved because it let out some strong feelings.

In all other aspects of his life, Kelly tried to be happy. He was in Little League, which gave him a feeling that he could overcome his clumsiness and be part of a team. He was in Cub Scouts, but that didn't work out as well. Most of the activities revolved around the kids' relationships with their fathers.

Kel's dad agreed to come to Baltimore so they could go together on a Scout camping trip. But it was cold and his dad decided they would come back a day early.

Kelly never went to a meeting after that.

When I started middle school I was a fragile kid with low self-esteem. I felt unpopular. Actually, I felt like a nerd.

When I was in elementary school everybody knew everybody. I was comfortable. But when I went into middle school there were kids from schools all around. I thought it was cool that I'd be going to school with teenagers. I started to like girls, but I was a chubby kid with curly hair so I didn't get far with them.

I became critical of what I wore. I had a huge urge to be accepted by the "in" crowd, and that's one of the reasons I started doing drugs. But I'll get to that later.

I really hated myself when I was younger. I was searching for something. I had to be accepted by the cooler kids. It wasn't too hard to be accepted because there weren't any official requirements. It wasn't a gang, but you just don't sit at a certain table in the cafeteria without knowing you're accepted there.

I used to sit with all my old friends at lunch. Then one day I sat with the freaks, people who smoke pot or do other drugs, wear whatever they feel like, and say whatever they want. They worship heavy metal and rock and roll, and long hair is a *must*. I was accepted from then on. I guess it was a little easier for me than for others. I make friends easily.

Sitting at the freaks' table gave me a tougher image. I don't know if I wanted to be tough, but I know I wanted to be popular. I was tired of being a sped, a person whose life consists of reading books and watching TV. A sped is someone who's inexperienced with life's daily pressures or, in some cases, just as experienced as freaks but less able to handle it. I was used to being obedient to my mom and that didn't mix with the image I wanted.

I wanted to be seen as a kid who had a lot of freedom and partied a lot.

Well, I accomplished what I wanted, but I took it too far.

After a while I was popular. That surprised me. It really did. I thought it was cool that I was sent to the principal's office for goofing off. Unfortunately, other kids thought it was cool, too, so I kept it up.

Somehow I always manipulated my way out of a suspension or a phone call home. That much I'm glad for. After my first year in middle school I felt comfortable. I had the same feeling I had from elementary school, but now I was more popular and more mature. So I thought.

When I cut wisecracks or threw needles at my home ec teacher I saw it as a way to keep me popular.

I started to smoke cigarettes. It was, and still is, an image thing, but more then than now. As I've said, I'm an addictive type, and smoking fits right into the pattern.

Today it's really rough for kids going through the transformation from child to teenager. There are a lot of decisions to be made and a lot of roads to be taken. The hard part is making the decisions, choosing between right and wrong and weighing whether or not social acceptance is worth risking your family relationship and your schoolwork. But there is nothing more important than feeling at peace within yourself. The tricky part is figuring out how to make that happen.

I risked it all and almost lost. If I hadn't made the final decision to go into treatment, I surely would have lost it all. I'm lucky to be here. A lot of kids who read this book may try to pretend they think I'm full of it, but anyone who's partying as much as I was will know what I'm talking about. There are a lot of kids out there who feel they can control their drug use, and they can at the start. But then the use

becomes more frequent, with more potent doses of whatever the drug may be. Even pot. I used pot for two years before I tried LSD.

I eventually got bored with casual drug use and decided I needed to open up to the wonderful world of addiction.

CHAPTER 3

THE FIRST TIME

It took about two years, but life gradually became routine for us after moving to Baltimore. We found a three-bedroom house to rent because I thought it was important for the kids to have their own bedrooms.

Our house is on the corner of a small group of suburban homes in walking distance to a cider mill, the elementary and middle schools, and most of Kelly's friends. There are trees and a stream. I was excited that I was giving my children back some of the things we gave up with the divorce. We bought a dog and named him Odie.

I worked as a newspaper reporter downtown, so I dropped off Jessica at a day-care center near my office. By this time Kel was coming home from school by himself.

About a mile from our home is a shopping mall. I used to watch the kids who hung out there when I went to the grocery store, and I was thankful Kelly wasn't one of them. They were mostly boys in their early teens who wore black pants and jackets. They smoked cigarettes as they leaned against the lightpoles and tried to convince each other they were tough. They frightened me because they seemed disrespectful and unnaturally self-possessed.

I often wondered what their parents were like. Why would they let their kids hang out, looking like a comic rendition of James Dean? Looking back, I can hardly recognize myself in the woman who judged those parents, now that my own story so closely resembles theirs.

As he got closer to puberty, Kelly gradually lost his chubbiness. When he was younger, he couldn't catch a ball to save his life, but now he was almost graceful. He developed an avid interest in soccer and baseball and went to sports camps in the summer. He started bragging about his muscles and worrying that he was too fat, when in fact he was scrawny from about 11 to 13.

He changed in other ways, too. He had been respectful and close to me. We were good friends because we had shared the divorce and the rebuilding of our lives. He had a mature appreciation for the struggle we had gone through.

He began to argue with me. This new friction hurt my feelings, but I realized it was the beginning of Kelly's breaking away and I tried to accept that. I was glad he seemed to be gaining confidence in his physical and emotional abilities.

Kelly started talking about meeting his friends at the mall. I didn't think much about it until a Friday in June when he was 12.

Jessica was at a birthday party and Kelly was playing with friends. I was at home making dinner. When the phone rang I was startled to hear the security guard at a store in the mall. He said he was holding Kelly and a friend for shoplifting a pair of earrings and he wanted me to come to the store and talk with them.

Why would Kelly do such a thing? He was never the kind of child who would take stupid chances or let his friends talk him into a dare.

When I got to the store, Kelly was sitting on a folding chair in the security office. He looked at me as if he were afraid I was going to beat him, even though that was something I had never done. I wanted to now. But the look on his face was so pathetic I almost cried. He probably thought he was going to jail and this was our last good-bye. The guard gave him the standard lecture — he couldn't come into the store without an adult for one year; his picture was taken and posted on the bulletin board; and if he did it again the police would be called.

He promised the guard he would never shoplift again. His voice shook almost as much as his hands. As we walked to the parking lot, Kelly didn't have much to say, except that he knew he had made a mistake.

It took me a few hours to settle down, and I thought the incident taught Kelly that taking stupid chances is just that. Stupid.

I was wrong.

The call from the department store was the beginning of a transformation I hadn't expected. Kelly began seeing a new group of friends. They looked like the kids who hung out at the mall, but they were younger. They were tough and hard to get to know. Instead of sitting down and talking when they came to the house, they stayed outside. Eventually, Kelly stopped bringing his friends home, and I began hearing the names of strangers when he told me what he had done during the day.

When Kelly was 13 he had his left earlobe pierced. I tried not to be angry and figured if that were the worst thing he did as a teenager we would be in good shape. I decided not to try to explain it to my parents.

In retrospect, it's easy to see the gradual changes in Kelly as he entered puberty. At the time, I was puzzled.

School had been important to Kelly and he worked hard. Now he said school was just a place to be during the day. He had always loved to spend time with Curtis and me and Jessica, but now he started complaining when we planned activities, even vacations. He wanted to be with his friends.

Kelly became fascinated with hard rock music and he worried about his appearance. He stopped studying. I got calls from his teachers because he wasn't handing in homework and he was disruptive in class. Kelly said it was the teachers' fault because they didn't know how to teach.

We began getting mysterious phone calls during the night. When we answered, there was always someone on the other end, but whoever it was wouldn't speak. We talked to the

the police and the calls were monitored, but nothing ever came of that. Once, the phone rang at 2 A.M. and I answered it, expecting to hear only breathing. But a girl's voice said, "Do you know where Kelly is? You'd better check his bed."

Of course I knew where Kelly was! He was asleep and I resented the intrusion. As I got into bed, I decided to check Kelly just to prove that the girl was crazy. I went to the basement, which was Kelly's room, and quietly looked down. There he was in bed. The relief was like warm water rolling down my spine. I softly crept over to him and kissed his forehead. It was cold and stiff.

It wasn't Kelly.

My son had taken his pillowcase and blankets, rolled them into a ball the size of his body, and covered them up. Then he took the small panes out of the window above his bed and crawled out. I angrily punched the pillow, wishing Kelly could feel the blow.

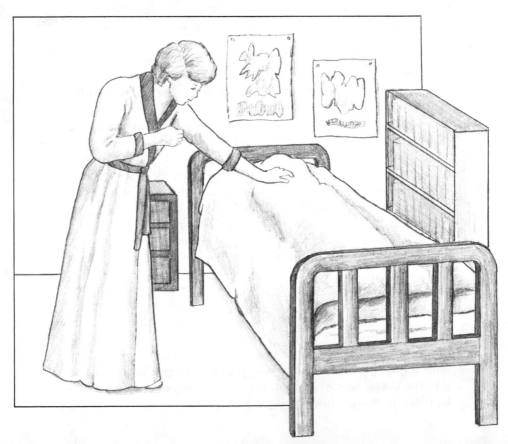

I replaced the window panes to block his entry back into his room. Now the only way he could get into the house was through the front door. I went up to my room and got my pillow and blankets. Then I settled onto the sofa. I didn't sleep. I sat still in the dark, waiting, for two hours.

At 4 A.M. I heard rustling and mumbling in the bushes outside the basement window. I went to the front door. As calmly as I could, I told him to come inside. As he passed I smelled alcohol and cigarettes on his breath.

I didn't yell at Kelly that night. I was too sad. I didn't like the stranger I was facing. Kelly explained that he and his friends had gotten a couple of bottles of booze and had a party by the stream near our house. They had shown him how to take the window apart so he could sneak out.

It was the first of many times.

When I was young I never defied my parents. I'm not sure why, except I couldn't stand to disappoint them. I had my first drink when I was in college. Kelly had his at 12. His need to experiment at such a young age troubled and alarmed me.

When my relatives asked why Kelly didn't want to spend time with them anymore I made excuses for him. I told them it was natural that he would want to be with his friends instead. I knew that was partly true. But I also knew the sneaking and lying were wrong, so I didn't tell them everything.

I was too afraid to face up to it.

I was about 12 when I first smoked pot. I was with maybe five other people. I'm not sure whether I did it because of peer pressure or just because I wanted to.

I remember the night distinctly. It was in July and I was with a girl I had a crush on. We went to this guy Tom's house. I knew there would be pot, but I went anyway, and I knew I probably would end up high.

I was scared to try it. I told everybody I had done it before, but I really had never seen the stuff. Something attracted me to it. Maybe just the fact that it was wrong appealed to me.

When I got to Tom's house we went to his basement and he pulled out this bong. I had some idea of what it was, but I didn't know how to use it. Everyone else was a few years older and I felt really insecure.

I had to smoke to be accepted into this crowd. I mean, none of them said, "Hey, man, if you don't smoke this weed you can't hang around us." But their thing was getting high and I knew I'd have to get high to be one of them.

So I was sitting on the couch and Tom started smoking a bowl. He passed it to the next person and so on. Then it came to me and I just took it. I was so nervous that I had a hard time holding the bong, but I managed to take three or four hits. I remember not knowing if I was getting high because I had never experienced it before.

I don't think the first time was the best. A lot of people say it is. For me, the second was better because I knew what to expect, but it was still a new experience.

Smoking pot is like breaking the ultimate rule, and for some reason I wanted to break it. The first time was fun, but it ultimately led to smoking at a more consistent level, flunking school, and more arguments with my mom and Curtis.

I had a tremendous urge to be accepted by what I saw as the "in" crowd. As I've said, it was around this time that I started to sit at different tables in the cafeteria. I started drifting farther and farther away from my old friends, and they began to wonder why I was hanging around the burnouts. I didn't know what to tell them. I still had friends who didn't use drugs, but I didn't associate with them as much. They are a cool bunch of guys and we had a lot of fun, but I had the desire for change. I wanted a new life-style. At least that's what I thought at the time.

So I started to smoke pot on a weekly basis. From there things started to go downhill. My grades dropped and I pushed limits with my mom.

I never really felt any guilt about things I did before drugs because I didn't have to lie about where I was going or what I was doing. But doing drugs and lying seem to go hand in hand. It's impossible for a person to be an addict and be honest. They don't mix. I started spending weekends at my best friend's house; we'd get high, and do pretty much what we wanted. I loved it. I didn't have a worry in the world. I just wish I could have foreseen the future.

I did a lot of things I knew were wrong and I didn't care. But later, I'd feel guilty. A little part of my relationship with my family was chipped away every time I defied them.

I no longer looked at school on an academic level. I was more interested in who was doing what when than doing homework and studying for tests. I used to achieve at a high level in school. In elementary school there weren't as many different classes of people — no burnouts, or preps, or punks. Everybody was friends. No one did drugs. It's interesting to see what the people from elementary school are like today.

If you had told me I would become a drug addict, flunk school, and go through rehab, I probably would have laughed at you and reported you to the school psychiatrist.

father. Yet he deeply resented not hearing from his dad on a regular basis.

One day that fall, I was in the elevator at work, talking to a friend who was upset. I asked her what was wrong. She said her 16-year-old daughter was having problems with school and she was concerned because her daughter was changing. I told her I understood.

A few weeks later, I asked her how her daughter was. She said they had found a psychologist and her daughter was seeing him twice a week, once individually and once with a group of other kids.

I got his name.

By the end of junior high school I was really treading water. Most of my time was spent smoking pot and having a good time. I've got to admit that I had fun for awhile. But I started getting high because it was the routine thing I felt the need for a joint or a bowl, and as soon as I own I'd want to get high again. And I usually did. en I started high school I didn't care about anything lizing with girls and figuring out how to cut my next out being caught.

d myself surrounded by drugs. I experimented my freshman year during the winter and late fall. try acid because I had heard wild things about bad things, too, but nobody ever listens to all ately, a lot of people find out the hard way how ly are for you. I started to use acid about once o, just before I was admitted to the hospital. e I tripped it was incredible. I walked about ggeration. It started at 12:30 A.M. I had so erhuman energy. I was with five other guys park about eight miles from home. When , I looked into the field and saw purple ter, I looked at the sky and saw the figures e Invaders" dancing. When I tripped, I

CHAPTER 4

THE ADDICTION

For a long time, I thought I was the reason Kelly had drug problems. I was convinced that if I hadn't been a single parent, he would have had more time with me and that would have made a difference. At the same time, I felt bad because my career was becoming important to me. After all, I hadn't gone to work because I wanted to, but I worked hard so I could have enough money to give the kids what they needed and deserved.

It's strange how many mixed feelings confronted me. I was angry and disappointed with Kelly, but guilty and frustrated that perhaps I had caused the problems. I felt inadequate at home as I became more accomplished at my job. I was down most of the time and took out my frustrations on the kids, for which I felt more guilt. For the first time since I was a child, I had temper tantrums.

During this time, Curtis became increasingly important to me. I was able to share my feelings with him, just as Kelly could with his new friends.

Curtis is an unusual man. I dated a couple of people after we moved to Baltimore, but they weren't interested in a new family. They all were divorced and had children of their own to worry about. I needed someone who understood that my free time included my children, and that one of them had a serious problem with my dating.

Curtis was never married, yet he was able to adjust to our situation with a good sense of humor and tremendous patience.

Kelly and Curtis met at the Baltimore City Fair when Kel was seven. I was working in one of the booths, and Kelly came along so we could spend time together. Curtis was working, too, and on one of his breaks he took Kel to the tent where kids could win a goldfish by pitching coins into a saucer. They must have spent $5 and never won a fish.

As we were going home, Kelly said he wanted to adopt Curtis. He changed his mind when Curtis and I started dating, and as our relationship became serious he saw us as teaming up against him. I often didn't have enough energy to deal with Kelly when I was alone, but when Curtis was at our house it was reinforcement. They often played ball together and we went to all of his Little League games, but as Kelly got older, they had less and less they could share.

One of the last carefree times Kelly, Jessica, and I had was during the summer Kelly was 13. All of us drove to New Hampshire and stayed in the home of a friend. It was on a beautiful mountain lake. We played Ping-Pong and swam and cooked lobster. I have a picture of Kelly from that summer on my desk at work. He's in his bathing suit, standing on the raft on the lake, flexing his skinny muscles. He has the smile of a little boy and the body of an emerging man.

That fall, Curtis and I began talking about getting married. He traveled during the week because of his job, but he spent most of his time on the weekends at our house. Curtis wanted to start his own photography business, which meant an end to the travel and more time with us.

One Sunday early in December 1984, we sat down with the kids in the living room and told them we were going to get married. We planned the wedding for the next June.

Curtis began to spend more time with us. When there was a conference with teachers, Curtis went too. He went to every school function. Jessica began to enjoy the attention. Kelly rebelled. The time Kelly spent at home became infrequent, and he turned increasingly to his friends for companionship.

Kelly didn't show much enthusiasm for the wedding. He was the best man, but he wouldn't go with us to New Hampshire afterward as we wanted him to. We were taking both kids on a trip after the wedding so they would feel they were an important part of our new family.

Instead, he went to Pittsburgh with his grandparents, Jess, and I stayed in the same house in New Hampshire as the year before. Kelly called almost every day, which made me miss him even more.

Ironically, a few months after Kelly stood during the ceremony beside Curtis and the minister.

Throughout that fall and winter, Curtis and Kelly remained concerned when school studying. He was a place where distractions.

One usual group smoking against going through

Another. They didn't felt that if he became

could see the music come out of stereo speakers, and — one of the trademarks of tripping — the walls breathed heavily when I looked at them. Each time was a new experience for me, but I admit that eventually I got strung out on acid and spent far more time crashing than anything else.

I'm lucky I got help. If I hadn't, a lot of bad things could have happened. Most drug abusers don't ever get the second chance I did. That's the sad part about it all. I'm lucky to have such a great bunch of people for a family. They've all been very supportive of me.

Before my hospitalization, I was so caught up in my addiction that when my family tried to help me I would turn it around and make it seem as if they were nagging me.

I started to resent them and picked on every little detail because I saw them as successful and myself as a failure. I resented that in them. I didn't know that was the real reason at the time, but it really was.

The Way Home

DRUGS AND THE FAMILY tells the story of one family's on-going battle against drug abuse, and many of the book's details are unique to the Martin family.

But the ultimate resonance of the Martins' experience derives from its universality, from the way they have crystallized a tale that is lived over and over again by contemporary families everywhere. Jo Martin could be any woman who must cope with the trauma of divorce, the relentless tensions between her responsibilities at home and her responsibilities at work, and the heartbreak of living with a troubled child. Curtis Martin could be any man who assumes paternal responsibilities for young children and links his fate to theirs. Jessica could be any little girl who must deal with a home life that is in a perpetual upheaval over the unpredictable and disruptive behavior of an older sibling. And Kelly himself is potentially any adolescent who seeks to "medicate" with illicit drugs his feelings of insecurity, inferiority, anxiety, and frustration, only to find that his emotional life simply becomes further destabilized by the ravages of drug addiction.

Yet on balance, DRUGS AND THE FAMILY is a profoundly hopeful book, because it clears a path from the mire of drug abuse to treatment and eventual cure. The Martins' great gift to Kelly was unconditional loyalty; their steadfastness in the face of all his provocations created the safety net he needed to seek help and follow through on his rehabilitation. Coupled with his family's support, Kelly's own inner resources and determination to get straight enabled him to begin the long process of creating a drug-free life for himself. The Martins' story is both a cautionary tale and an inspiration for all families beset by the misery of teenage substance abuse.

"Kelly's drug addiction controlled our family like a tyrant for nearly two years."

"For a long time, I thought I was the reason Kelly had drug problems . . . I felt bad because my career was becoming important to me."

Photographs by Curtis Martin

"Before my admission to the hospital, I liked to think I could handle anything . . . including drugs."

(Top) Curtis and I visited Taylor Manor one morning . . . What we came away with was reassurance that we were not alone with drug addiction and that they would try to help Kelly."

(Right) It was difficult to give Kelly over to strangers. But after an hour of intake interviews, he walked down a hallway and was gone."

"We were going to Taylor Manor a minimum of three times a week — Sunday afternoon to visit, Wednesday morning for family therapy, and Thursday evening for parents' group and visiting."

"My doctor was confrontational. He never stopped pushing. At the time, I hated it, but now I appreciate it a good deal."

"Whenever we were in the hospital, we had to ring a bell at the door to have a member of the staff unlock it . . . and doors were always locked behind us."

". . . he was beginning to accept Curtis, not as a replacement for his father, but as a tenuous friend."

"During the first two months, when we saw Kelly it was either with the therapist and social worker or at a table in the cafeteria."

"Kelly got special permission to go outside on May 4 so the family could celebrate Jessica's birthday at the picnic tables in front of his building."

"So much is different now . . . I've just recently been accepted into a good private school. I have a job and I'm even passing school. These are all things I thought were impossible in the past."

CHAPTER 5

TOWARD THE END

Sometimes, going through psychotherapy is like standing naked in a roomful of strangers as they throw cold water on you. It's awful. You're sure the therapist despises you as he or she pushes and prods and asks questions you want to avoid.

At other times, it's like an unexpected embrace. Psychotherapy is exhilarating because you can be totally honest with a person who won't make judgments.

Curtis and I were married four months when we started talking about finding a therapist for our family. Kelly wasn't the only one with a problem. Curtis, Jessica, and I needed to deal with our feelings of anger, frustration, and even isolation from Kelly. And, of course, he needed to confront his mounting addiction head-on.

We knew the kind of therapist we wanted: a man, so Kelly would be comfortable; someone near our home in case we had to go a couple of times a week; a person with an interest in adolescents; and a psychologist who would be willing to see the whole family.

Do you know how hard it is to find the right person? Imagine that someone you love is struggling with an emotional problem. Think of the tremendous responsibility you would feel to find help. And keep in mind that psychotherapy can be expensive. Our health insurance paid half of Kelly's therapy bills before he went into the hospital. That included an individual session and one group meeting each week and family therapy every other week. Individual sessions cost $75 for 50 minutes, group costs $45 for 90 minutes, and family costs $75 for 50 minutes. Those costs are average in the Baltimore area, and we paid half of that from October to April.

There are no guarantees with therapy. That's the one thing people told us over and over. When we were looking for a therapist I was director of the public information office at a Baltimore hospital, so I had daily contact with all kinds of doctors. It still was a difficult process and we decided the recommendation of a parent in a similar situation was the best indication of how good a therapist would be for us. So we decided to contact my friend's psychologist.

I hesitated to call because I had a lingering notion from my childhood that if you need any kind of psychological help you must be weird. Worse, I was afraid that the therapist would confirm what we already suspected — that our problems were more serious than we admitted.

After delaying for hours with silly excuses like getting a cup of coffee or going to the copy machine, I called the therapist from work one Wednesday in October. I told him our story, one he'd heard many times from other parents. It was a difficult conversation for me. We made an appointment for the next day.

His office was in his home, about five miles from where we live. It was on a shady street and didn't stick out as a place where weird people would gather. Still, I was frightened, despite his cats and friendly Labrador puppy and the feeling I was in someone's home rather than a doctor's office.

I answered his questions honestly. For nearly an hour I talked about Kelly, me, his father, and his sister. We discussed the divorce, my remarriage, Kelly's relationship with Curtis, his changed behavior. And then the therapist said he wanted to see Kelly. We made an appointment for the next Monday.

In some ways I was relieved that Curtis and I were no longer alone. We now had an ally, a professional with experience in seeing things we couldn't — and knowing what to do about them.

To my surprise, Kelly didn't resist the idea of therapy. Throughout his involvement with drugs he has been receptive to help, which is a good sign. He also couldn't deny the reasons we gave him for making the appointment — he was slowly pulling away from the family and replacing our support and love with relationships that included drugs and all their trappings. Lying, suspicion, cursing, anger, guilt, and breaking the law were the new standards in Kelly's life, and we would not accept them.

What made the situation doubly confusing for us is that Kelly wasn't always in trouble. There were still times when his sense of humor and sensitivity were alive and well and living in our home. He often hugged me and told me how much he loved me. There has never been a night in the last three years when he hasn't told us he loved us before going upstairs to bed. The exceptions, of course, are the nights he didn't come home. That's what made living with drugs hell for us. We never knew in the morning what kind of person Kelly would be when he woke up. Sometimes we loved him, sometimes we despised him for what he was doing to himself, and sometimes we were so beaten down that we didn't care.

Jessica was the person affected most. Curtis and I could talk out our feelings, but as arguments with Kelly became more heated, and as he became less honest, she complained of headaches and stomachaches. Her teachers called to say Jess's grades were slipping and that she was having trouble paying attention in school.

Who could blame her? The day Kelly stole my mother's car and was driving it down the busiest streets in our area I was upset. And so Jessica became upset. She had to cope with losing our attention, getting used to a stepfather, living with a brother who was changing, and trying to understand why there was so much tension every day.

In some ways, Kelly seemed to look forward to starting therapy. In other ways, he had misgivings. I'm sure he was thinking that maybe we would find out the extent to which he was doing drugs and he would have to face our anger, his guilt, and perhaps our rejection. He was powerless over his addiction but couldn't see that. Accepting help meant admitting there was a problem, which is one of the hardest things for an addict to do.

The one thing we knew for certain was that we would do whatever it took to help Kelly save himself from what clearly was becoming a need to self-destruct.

Before my admission to the hospital, I liked to think I could handle anything, including drugs. It wasn't really an ego trip. I just wanted to feel in control. Of course, that's exactly what drugs rob you of — self-control. But try telling that to an addict.

Still, when my mom told me she wanted me to see a therapist, I didn't give her a hard time. First of all, I wanted to please her. Also, maybe even back then I realized deep down that I needed help, even though I didn't want to admit it, even to myself. But, I couldn't tell you anything I ever accomplished with my old therapist, the one I saw before I was hospitalized. Even though I liked him a lot, he gave me exactly what I didn't need—freedom. I abused it.

By about the end of the second quarter in school, I realized that I was going to fail ninth grade if I continued to cut classes. Honestly, I felt bad about bringing home straight E's on my report card. But for some reason I didn't have the desire to change, and if I did I didn't have it bad enough. To tell you the truth, I never really got any help from anybody at school. I didn't want it, even when it was offered. I didn't give a damn about school and didn't learn anything that year. I looked at school as a social playground.

During the period of time when report cards came out and new classes started, I became depressed. I was losing all

of my energy. I had little or no willpower. And my addiction increased to the point where I *needed* to get high.

For instance, some of my friends and I were trying to figure out something to do one Friday night. The first idea that came to my head was "get high," but none of us had enough money to get anything.

That didn't seem to bother anyone but me. I flipped out. I felt I needed drugs just as though they were oxygen.

My drug of choice was marijuana. Besides marijuana and LSD, I did speed, downers, and painkillers. But those other drugs just didn't do as much for me as marijuana. Then again, marijuana never did anything for me in the first place. Let's just say I couldn't stay away from it.

That whole year went by in a kind of blur. I knew everyone was upset with me, and I wanted to fix that, but I was usually too stoned to pay much attention to anyone but myself. I honestly didn't understand how hard all my carrying on was on my mom.

I also didn't comprehend how much I was hurting my sister. I was so out of touch with my family and everything else that I didn't stop to think how badly I was disturbing them. It sounds mean, and it was, but I never thought of what kind of an impression I was giving Jessica. I think she was confused about what was going on, but now, luckily, we get along a lot better.

Hey, we still fight, but that's the natural thing for brothers and sisters to do. I'm actually glad that she's my sister. Isn't that incredible?

When I try to figure out why I smoked so much marijuana in ninth grade, I really don't come up with many clear-cut answers. All I can say is that it seemed to help me hide from the realities I was afraid to confront. I like to draw, and I used to sit in my room and get high and draw for hours on end. I thought that in order for me to bring out my artistic abilities I had to be high. I know now that was one big lie.

CHAPTER 6

THE LAST STRAW

As soon as Kelly started therapy, the psychologist wanted to know why we waited so long. The answer is because we're parents, trying to believe the best about our kids and assuming that terrible things only happen to terrible people.

A counselor must respect the strict code of confidentiality between himself and his patient. Otherwise, the patient will be afraid to work through his problems because his family or friends might find out about thoughts and feelings that are extremely personal.

Kelly's therapist confided in us only when a session with him was so serious that we needed to make a decision about what to do next. That's how we found out Kelly was dealing drugs, that his abuse was daily, that he seemed to want to medicate himself from life for some reason. All of those revelations were shocking to us, but not surprising as we look back on them. They helped us prepare for the eventuality of placing him in a psychiatric hospital.

Kelly met with the psychologist every Monday afternoon. Generally, Curtis dropped him off and I picked him up. More than once it made me sad that while most parents were arranging transportation to football practice or music lessons, our calendars revolved around visits to the therapist. What we quickly learned is that a lot of those parents couldn't face up to the fact that their kids had the same problems as Kelly.

On Tuesday, there was a session with other patients Kelly's age. Every other Saturday, we went as a family. Kelly told us little about his hours of therapy, but he became attached to the therapist right away because he didn't treat him like a child and allowed him to smoke when he wanted. We have a rule against smoking in the house.

Group therapy seemed to be the most difficult, yet the most important sessions for Kelly. The kids pushed each other because they all were in the same basic situation — one or two had been hospitalized, some had been arrested, and each of them had a serious emotional problem revolving around substance abuse.

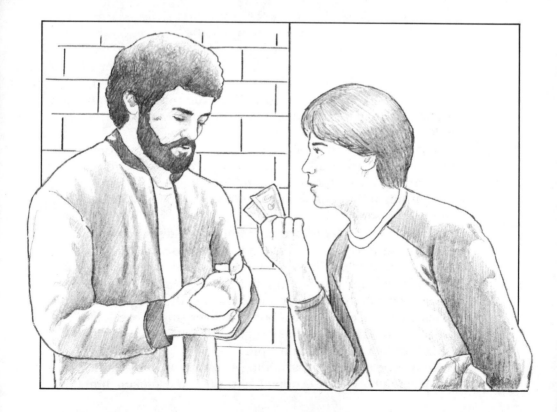

The therapist was alarmed at several things. First, Kelly was stoned during most of their meetings. We all were surprised he could use drugs like pot and speed daily and still function as well as he did. Some days he got stoned on the way to school, during school, after school and before he went to bed. The times he took LSD were obvious because his personality was radically altered. He never took it at home and rarely was home during its aftermath. But he was irritable, with a wild kind of squint in his eyes. He paced and couldn't concentrate. When he came down, he went to sleep and it was impossible to wake him. He slept for 10 or 12 hours at a time and didn't notice any of the noises in the house. When he took pot, however, he was mellow and pleasant. It took a stranger — and a professional — to educate us about the signs of drug abuse.

The second thing he was worried about was Kelly's lack of concern that he was failing school, that his role in the family was as adversary, or that he appeared to be heading for experimentation with more serious drugs. Things like PCP and cocaine. Kelly had no fear of heavy drugs and in fact seemed to look forward to seeing how they would make him feel.

Kelly didn't seem to want to change a thing, although he would tell us what we wanted to hear during a session.

"We can't get you to help around the house," we would say.

"You're right. I'll change starting next Saturday."

On Saturday he couldn't get out of bed.

"You haven't done homework in weeks," we'd complain.

"It's boring and the teachers pick on me. But I'll try. I promise."

He forgot to bring home his books and once, when he did, he left them at the bus stop. Sometimes he said he couldn't remember where they were. He forgot the combination to his lock at school, so he left his things in friends' lockers.

"Your abusive language creates bad feeling," we'd admonish.

"You're right. I get angry and don't handle it well. I'll stop. I promise I'll try."

Within hours he was calling Jessica a bitch. Or he would grab her arm and twist it until she screamed.

After six weeks of therapy, we decided to rule out any physical causes for Kelly's behavior.

A friend who is a physician examined Kelly thoroughly and found him slightly dazed and unresponsive to attempts at conversation. I explained he was in therapy for a drug problem and the doctor said he wasn't surprised.

The doctor ordered two tests. A five-hour glucose tolerance test would determine if there were an imbalance in Kelly's blood sugar, which would cause mood swings and lack of energy. The second test was an EEG, or electroencephalogram, to see if there were abnormalities in Kelly's electrical brain activity.

The glucose tolerance test is not fun. Kelly couldn't eat after midnight the day of the test. We went to the doctor's at 8 A.M. and Kelly drank a sugary solution. Then blood was drawn from Kelly's arm every 15 minutes the first hour, then every 30 minutes, then every hour, over 5 hours. I've had glucose tolerance tests and they're as much a test of strength as of blood sugar.

They hurt, you're hungry, and it's boring. Kelly didn't complain once, and his test results were normal.

The EEG, which is totally painless and easy, was a nightmare. It consists of attaching small electrodes to the scalp and having the patient lie still for about 30 minutes. The electrodes record electrical brain activity.

Kel and I were scheduled to go to the lab early one morning right before Christmas. When the test was over I'd take him to school. But he was agitated when he woke up, saying the tests would be used to prove he was crazy. He argued with me all the way over and didn't want to get out of the car.

Once we'd registered with the receptionist, we were told there would be a short wait. I sat down and began to read a magazine. Kelly wouldn't take off his coat and couldn't sit still. He paced in front of the other people and chain smoked.

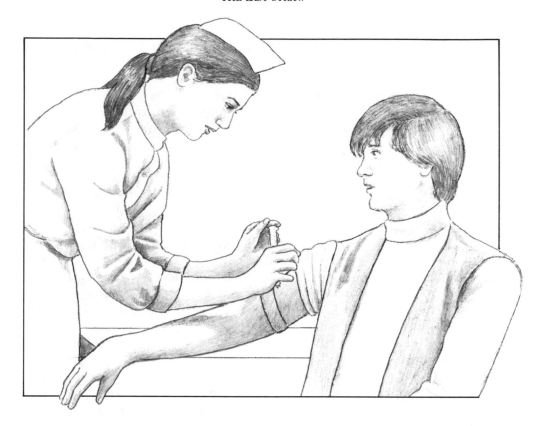

He reminded me of tigers in the zoo as they walk back and forth behind their barriers, looking for the opportunity to pounce.

I asked Kelly to go outside and wait because he obviously was so stoned that he would never be able to lie still long enough to have the electrodes placed on his head. And certainly the results wouldn't show normal brain function.

I apologized to the receptionist and said my son wasn't feeling well. I told her we would reschedule.

When I saw Kelly in the parking lot, I started to cry. I was angry and scared and tired. I told him to get into the car so I could drive him to school. He said he was too upset to concentrate and he wanted to go home. As we pulled out of the parking lot I started to scream at him. I told him I was tired of making excuses and being disappointed. I was going to do what I thought was right—to take him to school.

I told him what he did after that was up to him. I drove the short distance to school and let him out. He hadn't calmed down, although he was relieved he didn't have to have the test. I was sweating, despite the December cold.

There was no way I could go to work. I drove home with my heart pounding as I anticipated explaining to Curtis what had happened. We called the therapist and got his answering machine. We left a message for him to call as soon as possible. Then I called work and told my assistant there was a problem at home. I tried to sound professional, but I began to sob. She told me she would tell the boss only that there was an emergency. I could explain later.

Meanwhile, Kelly had turned around and walked away from school as soon as I drove away. He'd gone up the hill to the main road and hitchhiked to his girlfriend's house, where he spent the day. She skipped school that day, too.

The therapist called an hour after I got home. He told us to bring Kelly to his office that evening and insisted that

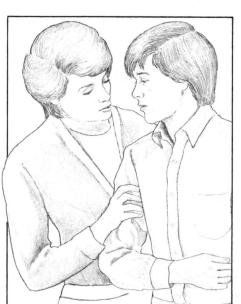

if ever he was unmanageable again we were to call 911 and have an ambulance take him to the nearest emergency room.

I never was sure what combination of drugs was in Kelly's system that day, but I'm fairly certain he was coming down from a long LSD trip. It was a pattern repeated later. In fact, it was only two weeks later that we came close to taking the therapist's advice and calling for emergency help.

Kelly spent a few days after Christmas with his dad in Pittsburgh. Just before New Year's Eve he returned. He often is down when he comes back from a visit with his father. The evening he came home he went to a friend's house. Curtis and I were home alone since Jess was at my parents' for the night.

Kel came home about 9 P.M. and was wild. His girlfriend told him she was moving to the West Coast. Kelly ran downstairs and then stomped back up the steps. He cried. He swore. He wouldn't let us touch him.

He made no sense as we tried to get him to explain what was wrong. He panted as he said he had to get away. The look in his eyes showed he was distant already. His muscles were tense and he spoke through clenched teeth.

I couldn't bring myself to call for help. The thought of seeing Kelly restrained on a stretcher in an ambulance was too much.

Instead, I convinced him to go for a ride. He and I drove for 20 minutes and then I parked near our home and just listened as Kelly told me how scared he was and how he was sorry for what was happening. He was totally sincere and totally helpless.

He said he couldn't live without his girlfriend and asked me why he chose friends who consistently let him down.

I didn't have the answers. I didn't have answers to anything anymore. It was the first time as a mother that I couldn't make my child's hurt go away. I held Kelly and we cried together. Why was this 14-year-old kid experiencing adult anguish?

Kel and I sat in the car for 45 minutes, the frost from our breath forming on the windows. We drove home calm and exhausted. Kelly went to sleep immediately and didn't wake up until the next afternoon.

I called the therapist from work the next morning and he said it was time Curtis and I began looking for a hospital for Kelly. He said Kel was doing serious drugs, more than likely to numb himself to what he saw as insurmountable problems and pressures in his life.

As we celebrated the New Year, there was a sense of dread rather than joy. Curtis and I had a quiet dinner together at home, both of us realizing without saying that our strength as a couple was the only way we would survive the coming year with the family intact.

By around Christmas time I really started to lose it. I was no longer the same person. My life totally revolved around drugs and the people who used them. I didn't care what the jocks and the nerds thought about me, I gave up trying to please my teachers, and I just blew off all my schoolwork.

Don't get me wrong. School was never really boring. Sure, the book work was, but socially it was fun. That's the only reason I ever went to school. Okay, I did some work, but never any homework, rarely classwork, and I failed just about all my tests. I failed every class in my first three quarters of high school. I cut school a lot. I would meet one or two of my friends before school and get very high off pot. Then we'd start to walk to school, only to say "screw it" and turn around because we wanted to get high again. We were so negative about life that there seemed to be no way to get into trouble, and if we did we didn't care.

Even though I had always cared about my progress in school, by this point in my life I was too caught up in other things to do anything about it. After failing those three quarters, I had a tremendous feeling of hopelessness and I wasn't about to confront my problems and work in school. I didn't have it in me.

I had an empty feeling inside that's really hard to explain. I'm surprised that I never thought of suicide. If I had really gone through withdrawal before I was admitted to the hospital, then it might have been a different story. But as long as I could get high I could keep going, and I never really had a problem getting drugs.

I live in a middle class suburban area, and every drug you can think of is easy to come by. The dealers aren't stupid. They know that all the kids in the suburbs have money supplied by "mommy and daddy." It's a natural market for them.

As I've said, I was doing a lot of LSD by the time I entered the hospital. In order for me to trip I had to get out of the house. So I'd sneak out at night, meet a few people, drop the acid, and go wherever it took me. I probably shouldn't say it, but I loved tripping. I'd walk for miles and miles. I had so much energy.

I'd see many different colors, hear many different noises, and think about many different things. I tried not to think about the aftermath — not being able to sleep, coming down, getting chills, and feeling depressed.

The acid usually kept me up until around 7:30 in the morning. I'd sneak back in at around 7 A.M., making all the noise in the world. It was obvious that I had been gone all night, but I didn't care. I was willing to worry my family and risk getting caught just so I could feel that high. I was a really sick person.

CHAPTER 7

THE BEGINNING

With the help of the therapist, Curtis and I made a list of what we thought Kelly needed in a hospital. We wanted a strict atmosphere where a smart kid wouldn't be able to talk his way around the rules. We wanted a place with a full-time school. And we wanted something close to home so we could visit and be part of the therapy.

We also decided not to tell Kelly that we were looking at hospitals. We weren't certain what he would do because he often threatened to run away.

We started calling hospitals to see if there was one that met all of our criteria. One near our home was too lax and Kelly knew someone in treatment there. Others were too far away for us to visit regularly.

We decided on Taylor Manor Hospital, about 45 minutes from our home. There were a couple of reasons. First, several doctors we respected recommended it. Second, there were strict rules and the kids couldn't progress until they learned that rules have a purpose.

There also is a full-time public school at Taylor Manor, which meant Kelly could transfer there when he was admitted and transfer back after discharge. His transcript would not show he had been in a psychiatric hospital.

Curtis and I visited Taylor Manor one morning in January. I was nervous because I had never been in a psychiatric hospital and certainly had never thought of shopping for one for my son. I imagined it was the same feeling a parent has when planning a child's funeral.

What we came away with was reassurance that we were not alone with drug addiction and that they would try to help Kelly. But there were no promises.

We also learned the charge would be $10,500 a month for room, board, and treatment. Our insurance company would pay 80 percent and we hoped the insurance from Kelly's father would pick up the rest.

All we had to do was decide when the time was right to admit Kelly to Taylor Manor. We still had a secret hope that it wouldn't be necessary, but every morning when we woke up there was the unspoken understanding that it was coming. We wanted Kelly to be a participant rather than forcing him into treatment he would resist. So we said only that we were looking at hospitals that could help him. He said nothing, but, as I look back, I'm certain he was relieved.

It is ironic in some ways that it was March 30 when Kelly asked us to put him in the hospital. It was his father's birthday and Easter Sunday.

He was sitting on the sofa after breakfast, trying to stay awake after being out most of the night. He was playing with a Polaroid camera, taking pictures of himself. One of them was the only picture I'd seen that was exactly what we saw when we looked at Kelly. He laughed and said it didn't look anything like him.

We had dinner with my family that evening, and Kelly looked awful. His clothes were wrinkled, and he had that spacey look in his eyes that meant he'd been doing drugs. He barely spoke all evening.

When we got home it was about 9 P.M. Jessica and Curtis went upstairs and I packed my sandwich for the next day. Kelly came into the kitchen for no special reason and looked at the picture of himself that had been taken at school the year before. It had been on the side of the refrigerator for all that time. He was smiling and happy, and his eyes almost danced off the paper.

Kelly went into the living room and got the picture he had taken of himself in the morning. He came back to the

kitchen and started to cry. He held the Polaroid and said, as if realizing it for the first time, "This really is me, isn't it? I'm not myself anymore."

I said, "Yes" and knew that the day had come. Kelly and I talked on the patio for nearly an hour. We both were scared. He said he had no control over what he was doing most of the time, and he wanted our help. If that meant putting him in a hospital, then that's what he wanted.

I reminded him that Curtis and I had looked at hospitals and there was one we particularly liked. I told him about Taylor Manor and tried to be as calm and reassuring as I could, given the magnitude of what was happening.

After our talk Kelly calmly kissed me and went to bed. I told Curtis what had happened, and we agreed to contact the hospital first thing the next morning to make arrangements.

When I spoke to the admissions director, she said a space would be available Thursday. You can't just walk in the door; you have to be referred by a physician or a psychologist. We called Kelly's counselor and told him what we wanted to do, and he called Taylor Manor to get the paperwork out of the way. It was set. We would arrive at 10:30 Thursday morning.

Kelly was unusually calm over the next three days. He collected his favorite albums and tapes and divided them among his best friends. He gave his jean jacket to his girlfriend.

On Tuesday evening, Kelly and I went out and bought him some clothes. We got toothpaste, a new toothbrush, and deodorant. It was almost as if he were going to camp.

But on Wednesday the dread I had managed to put off for two years hit me. I was determined to go to work and make Kelly's last day as normal as possible.

I haven't talked much about our friends, but they deserve to be mentioned. They made a difference in how Curtis and I coped with Kelly's addiction. Over a period of time we learned that our friends wanted the opportunity to help. Mostly, they listened. I started going out to dinner once a month with a friend from work. Now and then, Curtis dropped by a friend's house and stayed for a couple of hours.

Their listening helped diffuse emotions that often were raw. At times, Curtis and I were so frustrated by Kelly's behavior that we took it out on each other.

An example of how much our friends meant to us happened around noon the day before Kelly went to the hospital. My boss's secretary told me that we were going to have pizza in the conference room during our usual Wednesday staff meeting. I didn't think much about it because we did that now and then.

I was too tired and preoccupied to notice that something was different this time. The other six people on our staff already were at their places. As I sat down, I bumped into a giant blue balloon tied to my chair. On it was written the word *HUG!* At my place were pizza and soda, with a card propped on the can. On the outside was a teddy bear in a blue shirt, arms outstretched. On the inside, it said, "You look like you could use a hug!"

No one spoke. I read the personal note each of them had written on the card.

Things like, "Remember, if ever you need us, we're here for you." Or, "Our prayers are with you and Kelly."

I couldn't hold in my tears. I cried and tried to joke about losing control. "You know better than to be nice to me," I said to them. We all laughed and no one spoke of Kelly until I left at the end of the day. Each of them hugged me in turn, as if transferring energy from their bodies to mine.

That night, Kelly packed his suitcase, called a few friends to say good-bye, and then called my parents, who were on vacation in Florida. He was surprisingly mature.

"Granddaddy, you know I have a problem with drugs. Well, I'm going to get help," he said as he paced our kitchen floor. "The hospital is nice, Mom says. I'll be on a floor with girls and boys my age. And I don't think I'll be there more than two months. So you can write to me, although they'll read all my mail. Well, I love you both."

I cried silently, aching for my parents because I knew how difficult it was for them to be far away when their family needed them. I was certain they were as frightened as I was.

Then Kelly made the phone call that bothered him most. He called his father, talking briefly about where he would be and saying that the decision to get help was partly his. It was ironic that Kelly was acting like the father, trying to reassure his child that things would be okay.

When he hung up, Kelly hugged me, sighed deeply, told me he loved me, and went to bed. Curtis was upstairs, wisely leaving private good-byes for Kelly and me.

The next morning, Jessica and Kelly took pictures of each other on the front porch with the Polaroid camera that had started the week toward this incredible ending. She left for school with a hug for each of us.

Kelly put his suitcase in the trunk. He asked if he could play his Led Zeppelin tape in the car on the way to the hospital. I drove because if I had not I would have cried, and I didn't want to do that. I needed to keep going. Curtis sat silently in the front passenger seat. Kelly was in the backseat to my right. I could see him in the rearview mirror. His sunglasses could not hide the fear he was feeling. Occasionally, he wiped a tear before it could fall from his cheek.

His fingers tapped nonstop on his knees as he moved his head back and forth to the rhythm of a communion shared with the group he loved.

"Keep going," I told myself. "He's not the little kid you used to drive around the Virginia countryside. He's a different person. You're trying to get that other one back. That's why you're doing this."

It was difficult to give Kelly over to strangers. But after an hour of intake interviews, he walked down a hallway and was gone. Curtis and I filled out papers for nearly two hours and met briefly with the social worker assigned to Kelly. I liked her immediately because she let me babble about all the things she should do to help my son.

The last thing we did before we left was take his suitcase to the building where Kelly would live for the next seven months. We rang the bell, because all doors are locked at all times, and a young man answered. He said he would be Kelly's doctor and he would be in good hands. We smiled, said thank you, and drove away.

How hard it was to go from total absorption with Kelly's problem to not being able to play a role at all. It changed with the twist of the key in the lock as Kelly walked down that hall. We would have no contact with him for 14 days, the usual time families are isolated so the kids can adjust to their new life-style.

Curtis and I ate lunch in a small restaurant down the hill from the hospital. I couldn't be far from Kelly just yet. I drank a beer, something I rarely do. We talked about nothing in particular because we both were too preoccupied by a bizarre combination of apprehension and relief.

I got to work about 3 P.M. and tried to be optimistic as friends asked how the morning had gone. Curtis went home so he could be there when Jessica was finished with school. We said nothing more about the day until just before dinner. When I called Jessica and Curtis to come down to eat, I looked sadly at the table.

Out of habit, I had set four places. I felt stupid, lonely, frightened, and hopeless. I was more tired than at any other time in my life.

I couldn't make myself take away Kelly's place, so it stayed where it had been every evening for so many years. The difference that night was that we knew where he was and that he was safe.

I remember the day I was admitted to Taylor Manor. How could I forget? Everything was really dramatic. I was a scared kid. I had no idea that more than six months of my life would be spent in total rehabilitation.

To tell you the truth, I thought I was going to be in some sort of a retreat for about a month or so, but I was wrong.

I left for the hospital on a Thursday morning. I wanted to go to school and say good-bye to all of my "friends." I had mixed emotions locked inside of me that needed to be let out, without drugs. I had to learn how to handle life's everyday pressures without drugs, something I had no experience with.

I remember going into school and saying good-bye to my friend. He gave me a hit of speed. I popped it, said good-bye to him, and then just left. I'm telling you, I really was scared. I had so much on my mind. I had never felt like that. I just didn't know how to react.

By the time I got in the car with my parents to go to Taylor Manor, I was shaking badly. The speed didn't help. I

started to cry. I was just so totally overwhelmed that I gave in and tears started to fall. That was the first time I had cried like that since I was a kid. It felt pretty good. I was surprised.

When I arrived at the hospital it wasn't at all what I had imagined. It was made up of a dome-shaped building, the adolescent building, and scattered cottages. I wasn't sure what was going on, where I would be living, and who I would be living with.

First, I had to have an interview with my parents, a doctor, and my social worker. The doctor asked me questions like, "How frequently would you say you abuse drugs?" and "Do you have hallucinations often?"

I felt so strange because no one had ever been quite so up-front, so matter-of-fact, about my habit. Not even the psychologist I'd been seeing. After the interview I said good-bye to my parents. I wouldn't be able to communicate with them at all for the next two weeks.

So there I was, this insecure kid being taken out of a middle-class suburban area and put into an impersonal mental hospital. One day I was doing whatever I felt like and then the next day I was slapped in the face with a long list of rules and regulations that I had no choice but to abide by. If I didn't, I would pay the consequences.

That's the way things were. I had no say in the matter whatsoever. Boy, that pissed me off. I like to handle everything on my own, take control of everything. I felt totally helpless. If I tried doing anything physically or even verbally threatening, I would be put in a time-out room for as long as they said. The room was small and white with a huge restraint bed in the center. It had leather straps. It was quite intimidating.

When I walked into the coed unit, a tall, dark guy came up to me and took me into the time-out room and told me to strip. He then searched through all my belongings and asked me how long I expected to be there. I said one or two months. He smiled and told me the average stay was six to nine months. My heart fell into my stomach. I wanted to run, but there was no place or way to go. I was far from home, in the woods. I was so scared.

The tall, dark guy gave me a tour of the unit and introduced me to life in a mental hospital. I remember how shaky I was. I was just totally blown away by the idea of living in that place. I wasn't sure what was going to happen.

At least the kids were cool to me. One of them came up to me and told me just about everything I needed to know about the place. It felt better hearing it from another patient. It made me feel less alone.

CHAPTER 8

THE ROAD BACK

Taylor Manor is on a wooded hillside above an old mill town west of Baltimore, 36 miles from our house.

In the seven months Kelly was there, we visited so often that we drove 9,720 miles.

During the first two months, when we saw Kelly it was either with the therapist and social worker or at a table in the cafeteria. Whenever we were in the hospital, we had to ring a bell at the door to have a member of the staff unlock it. And doors were always locked behind us. It took all of us several months to get used to it.

Initially, we could visit for two hours on Thursday evenings and two hours on Sunday afternoons. Kelly got special permission to go outside on May 4 so the family could celebrate Jessica's birthday at the picnic tables in front of his building.

Parents of kids on Kelly's floor also met on Thursday evenings in the recreation room, and although it was hard for Curtis and me to get there by 5:30, we missed few sessions. The social worker was always there, and the psychologist and psychiatrist alternated evenings. Basically, the meetings were times to share frustrations and successes. They helped.

One of the first things Kelly did when he arrived at Taylor Manor was carve a cross on his right arm with a pin. Pins are forbidden because they're sharp, and any action to hurt yourself is considered a possible suicide attempt. So he immediately was placed on S.O.—suicide observation.

I think he had no intention of harming himself. The cross was a type of initiation to prove he could be part of the group. It didn't take long for him to fit in, but he resisted the authority of the staff from the minute he entered until he left to come home.

Don't misunderstand. Kelly wasn't a troublemaker at Taylor Manor. Far from it. In many ways he cooperated with the system. Deep down, though, he would not concede the right of the hospital to rule him. The more he learned to play by the rules — at school, during group and individual therapy, and at free time on the floor — the more privileges he earned. Eventually, the visits in the cafeteria were moved outside. We were going to Taylor a minimum of three times a week — Sunday afternoon to visit, Wednesday morning for family therapy, and Thursday evening for parents' group and visiting. Jessica didn't go on Wednesdays because she was in school, and she couldn't go to the parents' group, so she generally saw Kelly only on Sundays.

My parents visited occasionally, and they wrote often. Curtis and I did not miss a visit or family therapy session and we didn't go away for vacation the summer Kelly was at Taylor. The only time we almost missed a visit was a Wednesday morning when Kelly had a particularly urgent agenda for our family therapy session. About 10 miles from the hospital, my car overheated. By the time I pulled over the engine block was destroyed. A passerby called a tow truck and I went to the nearest gas station, but by then I was an hour late. I knew Kelly would be furious.

I called the hospital and explained what was wrong. I had no car and no way to talk to my son because I couldn't call him. He had to go back to class wondering what had happened and I had to go to work wondering what was on his mind.

My boss told me to call the doctor and tell him I was coming back. She gave me the afternoon off and a friend gave me the keys to her car. I left again and made the 40-minute ride to the hospital for the second time that day. As it turned out, the session was a good one. Once again I was grateful for friends who came through in a crunch. They never let us down.

Eventually, Kelly could leave the campus. After four months in the hospital we could take him to a nearby mall for dinner and shopping. He loved the stimulation of the lights and crowds after being isolated around the clock.

We learned early on that Kelly's progress would not be consistent. There were times when he was so frustrated at being locked in that he would pound his fists and cry. Other times he felt so close to his friends there that he didn't want to think of leaving.

There were high points and low. The lowest was when he admitted taking tranquilizers from my purse on a visit two months after he'd been in the hospital. One of the highs was when he was elected president of his unit.

Kelly was on the baseball team that played all summer at other hospitals. Sometimes they stopped for dinner on the way home, and he was happy the bus didn't say Taylor Manor because he didn't want people to know he was in an institution.

Curtis and I went to some of his games because it gave us extra time with him. We couldn't sit with him or talk, but we could watch him play ball.

We also started going to NarAnon, the support group for families of addicts. We went on Tuesday evenings and promised ourselves that we would attend six meetings before we decided if we would keep going.

After a few weeks, we figured that although it was helpful for most of the people there to openly and anonymously talk about their loved ones and the way drugs were ruining their lives, Curtis and I had trouble opening up among strangers. Maybe that's because we have such strong support from family and friends. We stopped going.

By early fall we knew Kelly would be home before Christmas. "The date" was the overriding goal, and he talked about it constantly. His therapist told us Kelly would be ready by the end of October, and we started making arrangements for him to go back to school.

We had misgivings about his seeing old friends. We wanted to get him away from his drug contacts. But he had a need to prove he had overcome the darkness of addiction and he asked to return to his old school.

In the month before he was released, Kelly was allowed to spend a Sunday afternoon at home. He was more nervous than the day he went into the hospital. He had not seen his room, his dog, or any of his friends for six months.

When he got out of the car he admitted he was nervous. We left him alone and he spent most of the time in his room, listening to music. It almost seemed he was euphoric to be alone after so much time in a confined area with a couple dozen kids his age.

The first time Kelly spent the night at home was the week before he was released. By then there was no doubt he was ready to be part of us again. He had learned to control his anger by talking about it. He recognized his deep emotional frustrations with his father. And he was beginning to accept Curtis, not as a replacement for his father, but as a tenuous friend.

The date for Kelly's release was set for October 31 — Halloween. The doctor asked him if he had any reservations about leaving on a spooky holiday. Kelly laughed and said, "Are you kidding?" The doctor then asked him whom he was dressing as when he left. "My new self," Kelly replied.

We could pick him up at any time that day, but Kelly requested that we wait until 5 P.M. We rang the bell for the last time. He appeared at the door, his dirty laundry, tapes, posters, and suitcase in hand. His friends hugged him and asked for permission to walk him to the car. It was denied.

The sun was setting as we rode down the hill, past the restaurant where Curtis and I had eaten lunch that first day. I turned and glanced at Kelly in the backseat. He was looking over his shoulder toward the hospital, which had already vanished from sight.

He sobbed. "This is harder than I thought. Those are the best friends I'll ever have," he said.

We were quiet most of the way home.

The trips to Taylor Manor haven't stopped.

We go back on Sunday mornings for family sessions and Kelly sees his therapist on Monday nights.

Drugs continue to be part of Kelly's life and he admits he smokes pot a couple times a week. But he's doing better in school. He has a job and has been accepted at a private boys' school nearby. We are beginning to trust him when he says he's going someplace. He never comes home late and doesn't stay out without permission.

We have a long way to go. There is still anger and suspicion in our family. We have told Kelly that if he does heavy drugs again he will go into a 28-day treatment center. And if he still has trouble, he will go back again.

It would be easy to stop trying to overcome addiction. But there's something that keeps us going. Maybe it's determination. Maybe it's fear.

Maybe it's because we deserve better.

I never imagined I could be as close to a group of people as I was to the people in Taylor Manor. There was a certain bonding between us that nothing can replace. Of course, there were a few certain people I could have killed and not thought twice about, but just about everyone was like family to me. It isn't surprising considering I lived with them.

If I were to go into detail about everything that I experienced in the hospital you'd probably fall asleep. Basically, I had two group and one individual therapy session every week, one structured activity every evening and one during the afternoons, except for the days I had group therapy. Let's just say you don't have much time on your hands at Taylor Manor.

My doctor was confrontational. He never stopped pushing. At the time, I hated it, but now I appreciate it a great deal. There was no other way to make me realize my problems. They had to repeatedly make me face my issues, probing my mind. I hated it, but I was going through such a period of denial — refusing to see that I even *had* a drug problem — that there was no other way.

After about a month in Taylor Manor, my roommates and I decided to carve crosses on our arms with a small pin, just for the hell of it. It was not done to hurt ourselves in any way. We were just trying to make a statement because

we thought we were tough. I even put alcohol on it after-wards to make sure no infection set in. The staff really over-reacted, if you ask me.

The place was, at times, like a prison. Thick screens on every window, backed with thick plastic windows that were impenetrable. Locks on every door, to which I had no keys.

I grew to love the staff that worked with me. They acted as my parents for those months, which seemed like years. I really learned a lot in there about myself and my family. It's hard to admit, but I actually did grow from that experience, and I do feel like a better person today because of it.

The day I got my discharge date is one of my happiest memories, except for the day I left, which was even better. Man, I'm telling you, after living in one of those places for a while you start to realize how frequently people take life for granted. Believe me, you think a lot in that place. They give you plenty of time to do that because that's what they want you to do.

Before I went in, I never really had any time to think. I was so caught up in it all that I just didn't realize what I had been doing to myself and the people I cared about.

I went through a period that all newcomers go through. It's called denial. What a word. I hate it. I wouldn't admit that anything was bothering me, or that I had any kind of problem. Little did I realize they had already heard it all a thousand times. I was trapped, held against my will. That's all I could think. Then I eventually realized it wouldn't do any good to sit on my butt and feel sorry for myself, so I actually started to work.

The therapy sessions began to go more smoothly. The truth hurts, and I had a lot to face up to, believe me. I owe a lot to my doctor for being such a good listener and always being there for me. Sometimes I forget how much I care for him. I got pushed around a lot. But in a positive way, even though at the time, I didn't think of it that way.

Looking back, I see that I got a lot of support at Taylor Manor. Someone was always there for me — a doctor, one of the other kids, my parents. I feel good about that. It also helps to know I can always count on my parents.

I went through many painful times in Taylor Manor, but I am glad to be able to say that every one of them was worth it. I mean that. I have no idea what would have become of me if I had not gotten help from my family and therapist.

So much is different now. I mean, I've just recently been accepted into a good private school. I have a job and I'm even passing school. These are all things I thought were impossible in the past.

While I was in the hospital, I never thought I could ever go back to partying, but three days after I got out of the hospital, I got high. And I still smoke dope occasionally. There are certain types of people who know they can never do drugs because their addictive patterns are so strong it would finish them. I know a few people who can handle it, but I would never, ever recommend it. I am trying mostly to steer clear of drugs. I never again want to be in the shape I was in before I entered the hospital.

My advice to other teenagers would be to watch someone you know who gets high on a regular basis, and see if he looks happy. I mean really look and ask yourself if you would like to live that person's life. I would also tell them not to fall for all the b.s. that addicts give about drug abuse. They glorify drugs and make excuses for them. It's all phony.

APPENDIX

State Agencies
for the Prevention and Treatment
of Drug Abuse

ALABAMA
Department of Mental Health
Division of Mental Illness and
   Substance Abuse Community
   Programs
200 Interstate Park Drive
P.O. Box 3710
Montgomery, AL 36193
(205) 271-9253

ALASKA
Department of Health and Social
   Services
Office of Alcoholism and Drug
   Abuse
Pouch H-05-F
Juneau, AK 99811
(907) 586-6201

ARIZONA
Department of Health Services
Division of Behavioral Health
   Services
Bureau of Community Services
Alcohol Abuse and Alcoholism
   Section
2500 East Van Buren
Phoenix, AZ 85008
(602) 255-1238

Department of Health Services
Division of Behavioral Health
   Services
Bureau of Community Services
Drug Abuse Section
2500 East Van Buren
Phoenix, AZ 85008
(602) 255-1240

ARKANSAS
Department of Human Services
Office of Alcohol and Drug Abuse
   Prevention
1515 West 7th Avenue
Suite 310
Little Rock, AR 72202
(501) 371-2603

CALIFORNIA
Department of Alcohol and Drug
   Abuse
111 Capitol Mall
Sacramento, CA 95814
(916) 445-1940

COLORADO
Department of Health
Alcohol and Drug Abuse Division
4210 East 11th Avenue
Denver, CO 80220
(303) 320-6137

CONNECTICUT
Alcohol and Drug Abuse
   Commission
999 Asylum Avenue
3rd Floor
Hartford, CT 06105
(203) 566-4145

DELAWARE
Division of Mental Health
Bureau of Alcoholism and Drug
   Abuse
1901 North Dupont Highway
Newcastle, DE 19720
(302) 421-6101

DISTRICT OF COLUMBIA
Department of Human Services
Office of Health Planning and
   Development
601 Indiana Avenue, NW
Suite 500
Washington, D.C. 20004
(202) 724-5641

FLORIDA
Department of Health and
   Rehabilitative Services
Alcoholic Rehabilitation Program
1317 Winewood Boulevard
Room 187A
Tallahassee, FL 32301
(904) 488-0396

Department of Health and
   Rehabilitative Services
Drug Abuse Program
1317 Winewood Boulevard
Building 6, Room 155
Tallahassee, FL 32301
(904) 488-0900

GEORGIA
Department of Human Resources
Division of Mental Health and
   Mental Retardation
Alcohol and Drug Section
618 Ponce De Leon Avenue, NE
Atlanta, GA 30365-2101
(404) 894-4785

HAWAII
Department of Health
Mental Health Division
Alcohol and Drug Abuse Branch
1250 Punch Bowl Street
P.O. Box 3378
Honolulu, HI 96801
(808) 548-4280

IDAHO
Department of Health and Welfare
Bureau of Preventive Medicine
Substance Abuse Section
450 West State
Boise, ID 83720
(208) 334-4368

ILLINOIS
Department of Mental Health and
   Developmental Disabilities
Division of Alcoholism
160 North La Salle Street
Room 1500
Chicago, IL 60601
(312) 793-2907

Illinois Dangerous Drugs
   Commission
300 North State Street
Suite 1500
Chicago, IL 60610
(312) 822-9860

INDIANA
Department of Mental Health
Division of Addiction Services
429 North Pennsylvania Street
Indianapolis, IN 46204
(317) 232-7816

IOWA
Department of Substance Abuse
505 5th Avenue
Insurance Exchange Building
Suite 202
Des Moines, IA 50319
(515) 281-3641

KANSAS
Department of Social Rehabilitation
Alcohol and Drug Abuse Services
2700 West 6th Street
Biddle Building
Topeka, KS 66606
(913) 296-3925

KENTUCKY
Cabinet for Human Resources
Department of Health Services
Substance Abuse Branch
275 East Main Street
Frankfort, KY 40601
(502) 564-2880

LOUISIANA
Department of Health and Human
    Resources
Office of Mental Health and
    Substance Abuse
655 North 5th Street
P.O. Box 4049
Baton Rouge, LA 70821
(504) 342-2565

MAINE
Department of Human Services
Office of Alcoholism and Drug
    Abuse Prevention
Bureau of Rehabilitation
32 Winthrop Street
Augusta, ME 04330
(207) 289-2781

MARYLAND
Alcoholism Control Administration
201 West Preston Street
Fourth Floor
Baltimore, MD 21201
(301) 383-2977

State Health Department
Drug Abuse Administration
201 West Preston Street
Baltimore, MD 21201
(301) 383-3312

MASSACHUSETTS
Department of Public Health
Division of Alcoholism
755 Boylston Street
Sixth Floor
Boston, MA 02116
(617) 727-1960

Department of Public Health
Division of Drug Rehabilitation
600 Washington Street
Boston, MA 02114
(617) 727-8617

MICHIGAN
Department of Public Health
Office of Substance Abuse Services
3500 North Logan Street
P.O. Box 30035
Lansing, MI 48909
(517) 373-8603

MINNESOTA
Department of Public Welfare
Chemical Dependency Program
    Division
Centennial Building
658 Cedar Street
4th Floor
Saint Paul, MN 55155
(612) 296-4614

MISSISSIPPI
Department of Mental Health
Division of Alcohol and Drug Abuse
1102 Robert E. Lee Building
Jackson, MS 39201
(601) 359-1297

MISSOURI
Department of Mental Health
Division of Alcoholism and Drug
    Abuse
2002 Missouri Boulevard
P.O. Box 687
Jefferson City, MO 65102
(314) 751-4942

MONTANA
Department of Institutions
Alcohol and Drug Abuse Division
1539 11th Avenue
Helena, MT 59620
(406) 449-2827

NEBRASKA
Department of Public Institutions
Division of Alcoholism and Drug
Abuse
801 West Van Dorn Street
P.O. Box 94728
Lincoln, NB 68509
(402) 471-2851, Ext. 415

NEVADA
Department of Human Resources
Bureau of Alcohol and Drug Abuse
505 East King Street
Carson City, NV 89710
(702) 885-4790

NEW HAMPSHIRE
Department of Health and Welfare
Office of Alcohol and Drug Abuse
  Prevention
Hazen Drive
Health and Welfare Building
Concord, NH 03301
(603) 271-4627

NEW JERSEY
Department of Health
Division of Alcoholism
129 East Hanover Street CN 362
Trenton, NJ 08625
(609) 292-8949

Department of Health
Division of Narcotic and Drug
  Abuse Control
129 East Hanover Street CN 362
Trenton, NJ 08625
(609) 292-8949

NEW MEXICO
Health and Environment Department
Behavioral Services Division
Substance Abuse Bureau
725 Saint Michaels Drive
P.O. Box 968
Santa Fe, NM 87503
(505) 984-0020, Ext. 304

NEW YORK
Division of Alcoholism and Alcohol
  Abuse
194 Washington Avenue
Albany, NY 12210
(518) 474-5417

Division of Substance Abuse
  Services
Executive Park South
Box 8200
Albany, NY 12203
(518) 457-7629

NORTH CAROLINA
Department of Human Resources
Division of Mental Health, Mental
  Retardation and Substance Abuse
  Services
Alcohol and Drug Abuse Services
325 North Salisbury Street
Albemarle Building
Raleigh, NC 27611
(919) 733-4670

NORTH DAKOTA
Department of Human Services
Division of Alcoholism and Drug
  Abuse
State Capitol Building
Bismarck, ND 58505
(701) 224-2767

OHIO
Department of Health
Division of Alcoholism
246 North High Street
P.O. Box 118
Columbus, OH 43216
(614) 466-3543

Department of Mental Health
Bureau of Drug Abuse
65 South Front Street
Columbus, OH 43215
(614) 466-9023

OKLAHOMA
Department of Mental Health
Alcohol and Drug Programs
4545 North Lincoln Boulevard
Suite 100 East Terrace
P.O. Box 53277
Oklahoma City, OK 73152
(405) 521-0044

OREGON
Department of Human Resources
Mental Health Division
Office of Programs for Alcohol and
  Drug Problems
2575 Bittern Street, NE
Salem, OR 97310
(503) 378-2163

PENNSYLVANIA
Department of Health
Office of Drug and Alcohol
  Programs
Commonwealth and Forster Avenues
Health and Welfare Building
P.O. Box 90
Harrisburg, PA 17108
(717) 787-9857

RHODE ISLAND
Department of Mental Health,
  Mental Retardation and Hospitals
Division of Substance Abuse
Substance Abuse Administration
  Building
Cranston, RI 02920
(401) 464-2091

SOUTH CAROLINA
Commission on Alcohol and Drug
  Abuse
3700 Forest Drive
Columbia, SC 29204
(803) 758-2521

SOUTH DAKOTA
Department of Health
Division of Alcohol and Drug Abuse
523 East Capitol, Joe Foss Building
Pierre, SD 57501
(605) 773-4806

TENNESSEE
Department of Mental Health and
  Mental Retardation
Alcohol and Drug Abuse Services
505 Deaderick Street
James K. Polk Building,
  Fourth Floor
Nashville, TN 37219
(615) 741-1921

TEXAS
Commission on Alcoholism
809 Sam Houston State Office
  Building
Austin, TX 78701
(512) 475-2577
Department of Community Affairs
Drug Abuse Prevention Division
2015 South Interstate Highway 35
P.O. Box 13166
Austin, TX 78711
(512) 443-4100

UTAH
Department of Social Services
Division of Alcoholism and Drugs
150 West North Temple
Suite 350
P.O. Box 2500
Salt Lake City, UT 84110
(801) 533-6532

VERMONT
Agency of Human Services
Department of Social and
  Rehabilitation Services
Alcohol and Drug Abuse Division
103 South Main Street
Waterbury, VT 05676
(802) 241-2170

VIRGINIA
Department of Mental Health and
  Mental Retardation
Division of Substance Abuse
109 Governor Street
P.O. Box 1797
Richmond, VA 23214
(804) 786-5313

WASHINGTON
Department of Social and Health
  Service
Bureau of Alcohol and Substance
  Abuse
Office Building—44 W
Olympia, WA 98504
(206) 753-5866

WEST VIRGINIA
Department of Health
Office of Behavioral Health Services
Division on Alcoholism and Drug
  Abuse
1800 Washington Street East
Building 3 Room 451
Charleston, WV 25305
(304) 348-2276

WISCONSIN
Department of Health and Social
  Services
Division of Community Services
Bureau of Community Programs
Alcohol and Other Drug Abuse
  Program Office
1 West Wilson Street
P.O. Box 7851
Madison, WI 53707
(608) 266-2717

WYOMING
Alcohol and Drug Abuse Programs
Hathaway Building
Cheyenne, WY 82002
(307) 777-7115, Ext. 7118

GUAM
Mental Health & Substance Abuse
  Agency
P.O. Box 20999
Guam 96921

PUERTO RICO
Department of Addiction Control
  Services
Alcohol Abuse Programs
P.O. Box B-Y Rio Piedras Station
Rio Piedras, PR 00928
(809) 763-5014

Department of Addiction Control
  Services
Drug Abuse Programs
P.O. Box B-Y Rio Piedras Station
Rio Piedras, PR 00928
(809) 764-8140

VIRGIN ISLANDS
Division of Mental Health,
  Alcoholism & Drug Dependency
  Services
P.O. Box 7329
Saint Thomas, Virgin Islands 00801
(809) 774-7265

AMERICAN SAMOA
LBJ Tropical Medical Center
Department of Mental Health Clinic
Pago Pago, American Samoa 96799

TRUST TERRITORIES
Director of Health Services
Office of the High Commissioner
Saipan, Trust Territories 96950

Jo Martin is director of communications for the Johns Hopkins School of Public Health in Baltimore, Maryland. She formerly worked as a journalist and editor for a number of years, and received her bachelor of journalism degree from the University of Missouri.

Kelly Clendenon is a 10th-grade student at a private boy's school in Baltimore, Maryland. He has studied art at the Maryland Institute, College of Art, and has a special interest in sports—baseball and football in particular.

Solomon H. Snyder, M.D. is Distinguished Service Professor of Neuroscience, Pharmacology and Psychiatry at The Johns Hopkins University School of Medicine. He has served as president of the Society for Neuroscience and in 1978 received the Albert Lasker Award in Medical Research. He has authored *Uses of Marijuana, Madness and the Brain, The Troubled Mind, Biological Aspects of Mental Disorder,* and edited *Perspective in Neuropharmacology: A Tribute to Julius Axelrod.* Professor Snyder was a research associate with Dr. Axelrod at the National Institutes of Health.

Barry L. Jacobs, Ph.D., is currently a professor in the program of neuroscience at Princeton University. Professor Jacobs is author of *Serotonin Neurotransmission and Behavior* and *Hallucinogens: Neurochemical, Behavioral and Clinical Perspectives.* He has written many journal articles in the field of neuroscience and contributed numerous chapters to books on behavior and brain science. He has been a member of several panels of the National Institute of Mental Health.

Joann Ellison Rodgers, M.S. (Columbia), became Deputy Director of Public Affairs and Director of Media Relations for the Johns Hopkins Medical Institutions in Baltimore, Maryland, in 1984 after 18 years as an award-winning science journalist and widely read columnist for the Hearst newspapers.